AmerAsian:

My Journey to Becoming Whole
as a Mixed Korean-American

QUILLKEEPERS PRESS

ISBN: 979-8-9868389-2-2

Published by Quillkeepers Press, LLC
PO Box 10236
Casa Grande, AZ 85130

This chapbook is dedicated to my brother.
You're super awesome! ☺ ♥

Preface

You are about to read some of the most personal, most difficult to write poems I've ever completed. These poems show one the biggest story arcs of my life: my journey to self-acceptance as a mixed Korean-American (or AmerAsian). It has been an interesting road, and this chapbook marks its end; I am thrilled to be sharing it with you.

Most of these poems are true outright (particularly those of my younger years), but some fall more into the "daydream" category. All the feelings behind them are true and accurate; I may have experienced the same realizations in a different setting. But they tell this overall arc in my life of self-acceptance. Part of that self-acceptance was fully embracing my Korean heritage, which I reference throughout this collection.

I also want to share that my parents were always helpful in teaching me and allowing me to understand my differences, and I appreciate their loving kindness more than words can say. But even though they were always there for me, we are individuals with our own unique minds, and outside experiences can have their own effects on you; they can subconsciously grow like wildfire and morph in different ways. I say this because I want to honor my parents, my family, completely. I am extremely blessed to have every member of my family in my life, and I love them wholeheartedly.

I am a lover of folktales/mythology and have referenced Korean versions within this collection. There are many versions of these stories, so I wanted to explicitly share where I read them, in order for you to have the ability to read those versions, if you choose to. The books are included in the "Works Cited" portion of this chapbook. One poem was also inspired by a piece from Li-Young Lee, who is an amazing poet that references his Chinese heritage throughout his works. He is an American also, so his work really resonates with me. I have also included information on where to read that poem in the "Works Cited" section.

Thank you so much for choosing to read this little chapbook, which is so near and dear to my heart. I hope you enjoy it!

The Beginning

An Emotional Journey

Sweet Self-Acceptance

The Beginning

Taemong

After Li-Young Lee*

My mother had a dream of me,
when she and I were one.
She dreamed of a snake
coiled on her belly.
It was her taemong, her conception dream, of me.

How Adam and Eve were so deceived!
A wily snake, the fruit of the tree of knowledge.
Introducing suffering on this earth.
A snake condemned to writhe about the world on its belly.

I was strange when I was young;
a half-Korean girl in a place with no other Asians or mixed people.
How the other children were so deceived!
I was no gorgon!
I was a human child — just like them.

I once had a dream,
where I warred against an amphisbaena.
One of its heads was bigger than the other,
and I managed to avoid the larger head's bites,
and crushed it with a rake into the earth.
The victory was short-lived,
as the smaller head bit me with vengeance.
I then killed the monster,
but was horribly injured in the process.

The great Cleopatra, ruler of Egypt,
left this world with the bite of an asp.
After I awoke from that strange dream,
successes and failures came,
the pains brought by the striking bites of life.

I became a new creature,
my skin shed to reveal my nature within:
I am a Poet.
I writhe about on my belly,
hunting for experiences,
hunting for words, to birth creations.
Satiating the hunger within.
My dream.

Could this be what the taemong foretold?

Inspired in part by Li-Young Lee's poem titled, "Water." It is part of his debut poetry collection, "The Rose." Additional details are located in the "Works Cited" section.

A Girl of the In-Between

I am a girl
of the in-between.
Biracial,
bicultural,
always stuck between two.

I have always known
I was different,
even when I didn't
have the words
to express it.

Not quite like my mother,
not quite like my father,
the first-born —
an Eve of sorts.

I am on a journey,
searching and yearning,
for my Eden.
A fitting place for a girl
of the in-between.

Taegeuk

I am like the taegeuk.
Red and blue.
My father: Scotch-Irish American.
My mother: South Korean.
Two halves to make a whole:
Me.
The red –
comfortable with this American life;
freckles and hazel eyes.
The blue –
strange and unusual to many.
The target of taunts and ridicule;
black hair and almond eyes.
Red and blue.
Two halves.
Together, making whole.
I am like the taegeuk.

Hanbok Princess

What if Disney princesses wore hanboks?
Icy blue for Cinderella,
bright yellow for Belle,
and a multi-colored one
for Aurora
(so her fairy godmothers don't have
to change the color of her dress anymore).
I could be Snow White
and wear a hanbok
of primary colors.
A bit of Korea
with the American,
just so I could see
a bit of myself in them.
What a nice little daydream it was.

My Collection

What are you?
Where are you from?
Are you Chinese?
Do you know karate?

You're not from here.
You don't look regular.
You're not Asian.
You're not White.

I wouldn't have known you were Asian
if it wasn't for your [black] hair.
You look just like Lucy Liu!

These are some of the things
I've heard before.
I collect awkward phrases,
like others collect seashells.

How do you like my collection?

Monsters Within

Kids can be so cruel.
When you're different.
When you're "new."
You become a target
of taunts and ridicule.

This happened to me a-plenty
when I was younger.
I remember being
the only Asian,
the only mixed kid,
in my early elementary classes.
We moved around a lot, too.
I was chronically "new."

I know what it's like
to be bullied.
I know what it's like
to dread going to school.
I know.

Fortunately, as time passed
and I got older,
the bullying stopped.

But words can sting,
especially when you're young.
They can seep into your skin
and grow like ravenous weeds.
They can take up residence within;
they have a life of their own!
They can morph and grow
into monsters, lurking
in the shadows of your mind.

They can become monsters
you carry with you
always.

My Collection

What are you?
Where are you from?
Are you Chinese?
Do you know karate?

You're not from here.
You don't look regular.
You're not Asian.
You're not White.

I wouldn't have known you were Asian
if it wasn't for your [black] hair.
You look just like Lucy Liu!

These are some of the things
I've heard before.
I collect awkward phrases,
like others collect seashells.

How do you like my collection?

Why?

Do you ever wonder
why you are
the way you are?
Was I created
to always
be in the middle?
Not quite one,
not quite the other.
Surely there must be
a purpose,
a reason.
Something I must go through,
experience,
to share with others.
Something profound —
it must be!
That has to be why
I am the way
I am.
There has to be a reason
why I am
the way I am.

Coincidence

From the land of my mother's ancestors,
a story of a woodcutter
who steals the robe of feathers
of a beautiful bathing fairy
and makes her his wife.
After being married for a time
and having children,
the husband felt sorry for his wife,
and returned her beautiful
robe of feathers.
She then flew away with their children,
leaving the poor man in tears.

From the land of my father's ancestors,
A story of a regular man,
who steals the seal-skin
of a beautiful bathing selkie
and makes her his wife.
After being married for a time
and having children,
the husband felt sorry for his wife,
and returned her beautiful
selkie seal-skin.
She then swims away with their children,
leaving the poor man in tears.

A coincidence?

Maybe.

Maybe it was all meant to happen.

Maybe it was all meant to be.

*This poem was inspired by the story "The Fairy and the Woodcutter" in the book titled "Korean Stories for Language Learners: Traditional Folktales in Korean and English" written by Julie Damron and EunSun Yoo. Additional details are located in the "Works Cited" section.

K-pop = More Than Music

K-pop is more to me
than fun music,
and intricate dance moves.
I remember discovering it
as a teenager,
when my mom brought home
a VHS tape of a Korean music show
from the local Korean grocery store.
There was no YouTube then.
Only the Korean grocery store
with its rows and rows of taped Korean shows.

I wanted to know what Korean kids my age
thought was cool.
What music do they listen to?
What style of clothing do they wear?
Through that tape and others,
I learned of different groups and songs,
found a few favorites,
and bought a few CD's.

Through those tapes
from the Korean grocery store,
I got to learn a lot about "young" South Korea.
It gave me a tangible way
to learn more about Korean culture
and ultimately learn more,
and be more accepting of myself.

K-pop is more than music to me.
It opened up a world,
a lifetime,
of discovery.

Cherry Blossom Princess

Sweet and delicate cherry blossoms,
perfectly pastel pink,
like candy floss tears
falling from trees.

Little girls are like
cherry blossoms:
sweet and delicate,
perfect pink princesses.

I remember when I was little;
youth fleeting like
cherry blossom season.
So many things I wish
I could say
to the younger me.

Don't cry, little girl,
don't cry.
Don't let mean words
hurt you.

Don't fall, little girl,
don't fall.
Don't let the burdens of the world
weigh you down.

Everything will be alright, little girl,

tough times don't last forever.
Everything will fall into place, little girl,
you can - and will be - so much more.

You're beautiful just the way you are,
sweet cherry blossom princess.
Remember, little girl,
everything will be alright.

Celestial Sisters

The beautiful sun.
The beautiful moon.
The beautiful twinkling stars in the midnight sky.
You are fantastical sisters;
celestial wonders three.
Can I be your sister, too?
I feel the warmth of your rays,
the soft glow of your moonlight,
and the stars are like freckles in the heavens.
They match my freckles, too.

I could be the clouds,
floating candy floss to entertain you.
I could be the winds,
and blow a refreshing cool breeze upon you.
I could be the great expanse,
the stage for you all to shine.

I would love to be your sister.
I would love to shine like you do.
I would love to be a celestial wonder, too.

*This poem was inspired by the story "The Three Little Girls"
in the book titled "Korean Children's Favorite Stories"
written by Kim So-un and illustrated by Jeong Kyoung-Sim.
Additional details are located in the "Works Cited" section.*

An
Emotional
Journey

Dalgona

I wish I were dalgona...
I wish the dark parts of my mind could be chiseled away
like the shapes within the sweet candy.
Just remove all the anxiety,
the feelings that I don't measure up,
the area where sadness resides.
Leave only the sweet.
Leave only the fairest of dreams,
that make me burst with joy and love.
Take all that grieves me away!
Oh, how I wish I were dalgona...

Alone

I am alone.

A single cherry blossom flower,
fallen into a river,
floating nowhere.
Is it beautiful?
Are the petals soft
like velvet?
Is there a sweet fragrance emanating
from this single bloom?
No one can know.
This poor little blossom,
alone and unknown.

I can understand this tiny flower.

I am floating along a river of my own,
alone and unknown;
a trip nowhere.

Is my heart filled with love?
Am I beautiful,
my skin soft to the touch?

No one can know.

I keep myself hidden away.
I float along,
just like the little cherry blossom.

A Dokkaebi to Save Me

I need a dokkaebi to save me!
The bills keep rolling in,
and my bank account
gets sadder by the day.
Shower me with riches!
I'll share with you a drink.
We can be friends at a mountain-top home —
at least for a time.

Frankly, I could use a friend.
Times are lonely
when your pockets are empty,
and dark clouds hang over you.
Even if our time will be short,
a friend is welcome indeed.

Please, come visit me, dokkaebi!
I've worked so hard,
for so very long...
luck still hasn't come my way.
My mind is full of worry,
my back aches,
and my hands are calloused from wear.
I welcome you, dokkaebi!
Only you can save me!

Same Difference

Another trip to the grocery store…
florescent lighting, harsh and artificial,
and filled with foods
from all over this great big Earth
Walking along this man-made Garden of Eden,
I see it –
New and strange –
What is it?
A prickly large fruit,
oblong and awkward.
You, friend, don't look like the others.
A jack fruit.
You've come a long way,
from Asia to this American grocery store.
So did I.
We both have crossed the world to meet under
these florescent lights.
We both are different than those around us.
We both look out of place.
You and I
will escape these unnatural lights.
We will be like a modern-day Adam and Eve;
the same, but different.
Together, we will see the bright light of the sun.

A Parallel Me

Quantum Mechanics.
Decoherence Theory.
Radio waves.
Limitless parallel worlds.
Is there a world where I grew up in South Korea?
I like to think so.
A world where I speak perfect Korean.
I can make delicious Korean dishes.
I have married a Korean gentleman,
and have two beautiful children – the pride of their parents.
My parents, now honored grandparents, are so pleased with me.
My in-laws cherish me and are just as proud to have me
as their daughter-in-law.
What a nice thought it is,
this world I hope is out there.

Ready

I am ready to learn more
of my past, my ancestors,
the other half of me.
I will soar through the sky
like an eagle,
to arrive in the land
that has captured my imagination.
I have such love
for a place
I do not know.
I am ready for this journey.
I am ready to learn more.

Searching

I am looking
for something.
Searching high and low,
traveling to
the other side of the world.
Is it love, acceptance, growth —
Maybe one, maybe all,
I can't quite say.
I think I'll find it
in Korea...
it should be there, right?
I hope it will be there.

A New World

Being in this place is one of greatest dreams:
South Korea.
How long I've dreamed of walking on this ground.
A country so close to my heart,
but so far away.
Stepping off the plane,
onto near-hallowed earth.

So many people,
so many things to do,
so many little wonders,
in this place,
Incheon International Airport.
It looks like a set
in a sci-fi movie.
How beautiful it is!

The sights,
the sounds,
the smells;
some familiar, some new.
There are stores here I know,
stores I've visited before,
but here they are so different.
The Korean community is tight where I'm from,
but here, all these people are unknown to me.
This doesn't feel like another country.
Instead, it feels like another world.

What a rush of thoughts and feelings
in such little time!
In the midst of all this
pleasant chaos,
one thing is for certain:
this will be an adventure like no other.

Dokdo

One day,
I'll take my mom
to Dokdo.
The place she dreams of going.
The most beautiful
little island,
in the middle of the sea.

We'll ride the choppy waters,
and arrive victorious,
on the little island's beach.
Our prize will be the salty sea air,
filling our lungs and blowing
wild winds into our hair,
as we stand on the ground
so loved by Koreans.

But the greatest prize for me,
will be the realization
of one of my mother's
greatest dreams.
I long to see her smile,
the sun glowing on her face,
on Dokdo,
the place she dreams of going.
The most beautiful
little island,
in the middle of the sea.

Seoul

This is the place
I come from.
This is the place
that first met me,
as I left the security
of my mother's womb.

Seoul.
The city of modern wonders.
The city of K-pop,
dramas,
and fiery, delicious cuisine.

This is the place
I come from.
A place I am ready
to reintroduce
myself to.

A Bittersweet Return

It can't be helped.
Time has moved on,
and I am a different person.
I've returned to the place I came from,
but not my home.
A land foreign to me,
but still a part of me.
I've finally made it here.
I came to South Korea to fall in love…
to fall in love with the place that carries claim to me.
I came to South Korea to learn about my motherland.
Where I was born,
where my mother was born,
where countless ancestors came into being.

Do you remember me?
Can you still hear my cries
from when I entered this existence?
Do you love me,
as I love you?

It can't be helped.
This place does not know me.
I am not remembered.
Of course, I wouldn't be.
Of course, there would be
no place held for me,
just in case I returned.

But still, I hoped for something…
some kind of magic, I guess.

This country is still beautiful,
it still has a place in my heart,
and I'm still glad I came.
But something I was searching for –
a deep soul warmth, a near-magical connection –
didn't happen.
You are beautiful, South Korea.
I do love you, but something is missing.
I thought I could find it here,
but I have learned no place can satisfy this need.
I must complete a journey within.

Moon, Comb, Mirror

I see myself
in stories.
There's a tale
of a young Korean couple:
a forgetful husband,
and a wife who wants
a comb for her hair.
As he goes off on a journey,
she asks him to buy a comb.
To help him remember,
she points him towards
the crescent moon,
shaped like the object of her desires.
Unfortunately,
he arrives when the moon is full,
and buys her a mirror instead,
forgetting what she wanted.
The mirror causes chaos
when brought home -
the wife sees a "pretty woman"
in it and demands to know who she is -
and it is broken.

I see myself
in stories.
I am like the wife,
unable to see the beauty in me.
I am like the husband,

forgetting what's important.
I am like the broken mirror,
plainly misunderstood.

Yes, I see myself
in stories.
Now, I must
rewrite the one
I am living.

This poem was inspired by the story "The Bridegroom's Shopping" in the book titled "Korean Children's Favorite Stories" written by Kim So-un and illustrated by Jeong Kyoung-Sim. Additional details are located in the "Works Cited" section.

Namsan Tower

So, this is Seoul.
In the dark of night,
surrounded by onlookers,
it feels like it is only me and you, dear Seoul.
I hear others speaking Korean -
some words I understand, but most I don't.
Your lights entrance me;
this amazing wondrous beauty!
I am but a moth,
enchanted by flame-like neon lights.
The stars, the very moon,
must be jealous of your bright lights.
How they shine!
What a marvel you are!

To walk up this mountain
was like a religious experience;
a pilgrimage to a divine site at the top
of a holy mountain.
Well, I have been treated to a divine sight, indeed!

How amazing you are, Seoul…
an ocean of beautiful lights.
How you have charmed me;
you have won my heart.

Soon...

Dark days and disappointments
have crushed my spirit.
My tender heart has taken on
enough sorrow for a thousand lifetimes.
But even though I wallow in the mud
with tear-stained cheeks,
I can feel the tide beginning to turn.
Nothing lasts forever;
bad times will eventually cease.
I will have my time of glory.
I will become the hero
that lives deep within my soul.
I will be reborn in wholeness –
yang and eum –
perfected and made strong
through my trials and tribulations.
Soon, songs of victory
will be mine.

Sweet Self-Acceptance

Born Again

I am born again.
I am a new creature.
I have escaped
the cocoon of the past,
and like a luna moth,
I am rare and beautiful.

I am made of flames.
The fire in my heart
blazes inside my chest,
sending sparks throughout my body.
I rise like heat from a raging inferno.
I rocket into the atmosphere,
a stronger version of myself.

This is what I am meant be,
a being of beauty,
of strength,
of passion,
of bravery.
I will no longer allow my past
to haunt me,
to shame me into being small.
All that I was is dead and gone,
burned away into ash.

The present time is mine completely.
Now, I live the life meant for me.

No More

For too long,
I allowed others to dictate my life.
For too long,
I hid from the world.
For too long,
I believed I was less than everyone else.

No more.

I am like a haetae.
I've eaten the fire;
its flames blazing in my belly.
This fire is confidence,
burning away all the negativity within.
I will be born anew;
a woman entering the world
through the sacred flame.

Never again,
will I allow myself to be disrespected.
Never again,
will I hide within prisons of my own making.
Never again,
will I entertain the idea that I am not enough.

No more.

The Journey Within

You can change your environment.
You can move to faraway lands.
You can wander deep into wild woods.
But none of these
can bring true joy.
Yes, happiness for a time, maybe.
But your worries,
your pain,
your supposed "inadequacies"
will follow you wherever you go.
The journey within,
with a focus on healing,
a commitment to health
and cultivating self-worth -
is what will set you free.
That is what opens
the door to true happiness.

Two Brothers

A Korean folktale
tells of two brothers:
one, young and kind;
the other, old and greedy.
The younger helped a bird with a broken leg,
who one day repaid him by
dropping a magical pumpkin seed on his land.
The pumpkins grew large,
and were filled with incredible riches.
The older brother
became jealous,
and wanting to receive what his brother had,
hurt a bird in order to heal it.
That bird gifted him a magical pumpkin seed, too...
but it was filled with horrors
that made him destitute.
The older brother eventually saw the error of his ways,
and he and his younger brother lived well
with the riches the kind brother had received.

You could say the brothers got what they deserved -
what they needed to acquire for their growth.
Everything even worked out for the best in the end!

I can look back on my life and see -
I have also attracted what I needed for growth.
I believe wholeheartedly,
everything will work out best in the end.

*This poem was inspired by the story "The Pumpkin Seeds" in
the book titled "Korean Children's Favorite Stories" written
by Kim So-un and illustrated by Jeong Kyoung-Sim. Additional
details are located in the "Works Cited" section.*

Seolmundae Halmang

I want to be as prolific
as Seolmundae Halmang,
The great Grandmother,
The Creator Goddess
of Jeju-do.

How she created that
beautiful island
with her own hands!
A place of beauty and wonder.

How I hope to create
beauty and wonder
with these words I write!
Sharing parts of me
with my own hands.

Oh, how I hope to be as prolific
as Seolmundae Halmang.
How you are such a great Grandmother!
How I hope I will one day be seen
as akin to a creator Goddess.
How I hope my works will have
a fraction of the beauty
of the great Jeju-do.

Letting Go

There is a tale
of a Korean prince,
who didn't let go
of his childhood stories,
which grew angry and bitter
as he got older.
It is time I let go of
my childhood stories;
I'm not strange or weird
for my ethnicity!
I have no reason to carry
any shame for who I am!
There is nothing wrong with me.
I am an equal to all human beings
that inhabit this earth.
I felt inadequacies
as a child;
taunts and teasing
left their scars.
But I am an adult now.
My destiny is mine to create.
I am whole and strong.
It is time to let go
of childhood stories.
I am ready
to be more.

This poem was inspired by the story "The Story Bag" in the book titled "Korean Children's Favorite Stories" written by Kim So-un and illustrated by Jeong Kyoung-Sim. Additional details are located in the "Works Cited" section.

Honhyeol

I am half.
There were times
it hurt to acknowledge it.
The truth of me
was my greatest pain.
But now I love it and
appreciate it.
I know now
the truth of me,
is the beauty of me.
Even if a mystical genie
appeared before me,
ready to change me,
I would decline.
The truth of me:
I am half,
South Korean and Scotch-Irish American.
These two halves –
I see now –
make me completely,
totally,
fully,
whole.

Rare

I remember thinking
when I was young,
that people like me -
half-Korean -
must be incredibly rare.
No one else was like me....
well, no one I wasn't
related to.
What a strange feeling it was,
that on this whole planet,
there weren't very many
people like me.
Maybe there's still some truth to it,
though it doesn't bother me anymore.
Red and blue diamonds are rare, too.

Born in Half

There is an old folktale
of a son who was born
with only half of his body.
When he met a young girl
he wanted as his bride,
the girl's parents refused.
He later took her from the home,
and the next day,
he had a whole body!
Through this union,
his true love,
his body was made whole.

Through the union
of self-love
and self-acceptance,
I am made whole…
just like the son
who was born in half.

This poem was inspired by the story "The Half Son" in the book titled "Korean Stories for Language Learners: Traditional Folktales in Korean and English" written by Julie Damron and EunSun Yoo. Additional details are located in the "Works Cited" section.

Proud

Perfectly created, as all other beings.
Ready to accept all that I am.
Of course, I am more than enough.
Ugly behavior from others doesn't define me.
Dare I say, I'm beautiful, just the way I am.

The Bouquet of Me

Begin with mugunghwa,
then add some thistle
and shamrock;
these are for
all who have come before me.
Fragrant honeysuckle
and pine needles
will add a bit of flair...
magnolia, too!
These are for
the land I call home.
Add some daisies and daffodils
for a sunny disposition.
Finally, add brightly colored,
tropical hibiscus
(they're my favorite)
and you now have
a completed bouquet
of me,
Kimberly.

Amor Fati: The Love of Fate

Though pain lies in my past,
so do triumphs.
Some even born from
the hurtful experiences!
I now see
the connecting thread
in my life.
The difficulties that came,
which ultimately helped
me grow.
Amor Fati,
the love of fate,
I understand it now.
Through all of life's
twisting, winding roads,
I've found the path
meant for me.
I'm pushing forth;
I'm proudly on my hero's journey.
I love where I am going,
all because of where I've been.

I am American

I am American.
This is my country.
This is my home.

South Korea helped me
appreciate where I am from,
the culture I have grown up in,
so much more.

America has always been
precious to me,
but I dreamt of a utopia
that does not exist.

South Korea is also
precious to me;
I have learned so much
and am greater for the experience.

Sometimes, one needs
a different perspective,
some time away,
to appreciate where they are from.

What I needed,
what I was searching for,
was within me all along:
sweet self-acceptance.

This is my home.
This is my country.
I am American.

Snakeskin

Shed the past
like snakeskin,
allow yourself
to be free.
Let yourself grow
into the person
you're meant to be.

Taemong II

I've wondered about
the taemong of me.
Why was I not something
small and cute?
Colorful and sweet?
But now, I understand.

I wasn't created to be cute.
I am no flower,
I am no sweet fruit.
No, I am a creature
of transformation.
I have shed old skins,
old sins,
to become a new being.
I am born anew.
Death and rebirth,
rebirth and death.
The great ouroboros.

I am a creature of knowledge,
devouring books, information of all sorts.
I have learned and grown,
fought with my inner nature,
to be who I am today.

Of course,
the taemong of me
wouldn't be cute and sweet!
I am a creature
of transformation.
I am the snake.

Works Cited

Damron, Julie, and EunSun You. *Korean Stories for Language Learners: Traditional Folktales in Korean and English*. Tuttle Publishing, 2018.

Kim, So-un. *Korean Children's Favorite Stories*. Illustrated by Jeong Kyoung-Sim. Tuttle Publishing, 2004.

Lee, Li-Young. *Rose*. BOA Editions Ltd., 1993.

Special Thanks

I would like to thank my family for always being there for me. I am so very blessed to have you all in my life. Thank you for your continuous love and support. I love you all very much!

I would also like to thank my dear friend Serena Morrigan (@serena.morrigan on Instagram). She gave me thoughtful suggestions that helped me improve upon this collection. I'm so glad we have connected; thank you for being such a great friend!

Thank you as well to Stephanie Lamb and the Quillkeepers Press, LLC team (@quillkeeperspress on Instagram)! Thank you so much for publishing this collection; I am incredibly grateful for the opportunities you all have provided me! I appreciate you all!

Lastly, I'd like to thank you for reading this poetry collection. These poems hold a special place in my heart, and it means a lot to me that you took the time to read them. Thank you very much, and I hope you enjoyed them ☺

About the Author

Kimberly McAfee is a writer and poet residing in the US. She has authored/co-authored works in a variety of formats, such as websites, e-magazines, anthologies, and even a peer-reviewed scholarly journal. Ms. McAfee has also self-published three chapbooks, available on Amazon. You can find more of her poetry on her Instagram page @writerpoetkim.

What Others are Saying About AmerAsian

"Kim's AmerAsian weaves a tapestry of beautiful and painful personal experiences. Centered around being from two ethnic worlds, while tying it all in with multiple mythologies, Kim creates a touching and lovely poetry collection that teaches us all the power of finding your own way and then embracing it."

—Enoch Black, Author of *Incubus Tales*

"A thought-provoking tale of identity and accepting your place in the world. AmerAsian is a beautiful poetry book that explores, from many angles, the journey of growing up visibly different from those around you. The poet invites you into her world, to see it through her eyes, as a child into a self-aware adult. A lovely story was told throughout this collection and it will touch the heartstrings of anyone who has ever felt displaced by society."

—Emma-Jane Barlow, *Author of Sins & Sunflowers* and *Darkness & Light*

"This book encapsulates the experience of being both Asian and American in a world that often only wants you to check one box. It explores the identity issues that can arise but also the beautify of differences. As a mixed Asian American myself I related to poem after poem in this book. The writer so eloquently delivered such an important message."

—Kyoko W.P., Author of *Big Feels*

"Through her use of vivid imagery and candid storytelling, Kim presents poems that openly explore her search for identity and self-acceptance. She not only takes you on a personal journey with her words, but makes you feel as though you're right there alongside her.

As a mixed person myself, I found this book very moving and could understand the struggle of trying to connect with each ethnicity, the feeling of being out of place and the need for belonging.

The last chapter was my favourite part of the book. It leaves you with the sense that there is power in discovering that despite past pain and insecurities, you can also find strength in your uniqueness and be proud."

—Elaine T. Stockdale, Author of *Seasons and Paper Hearts*

Other Titles by Kimberly McAfee

No Love Truer —A short chapbook of Christian poetry. It is meant to provide you with a bit of inspiration, and as a reminder of God's love for you.

Consumed — Inspired by passion, love, and romance, this chapbook contains poems from a modern romantic.

The Siren's Call — Vampires. Sirens. Psychological Horror. Curses. Mummies. Candy? Residing in this chapbook are poems encompassing many facets of Halloween - the sweet and fun - and horror - monsters and psychological turmoil.